The
Ruth Laredo
Becoming A Musician Book

EA 714

European American Music Corporation
Valley Forge, Pennsylvania

Great Britain: Alfred A. Kalmus (Universal Edition) Ltd, London
Continental Europe: B. Schott's Söhne, Mainz
Japan: Schott Japan Company Ltd, Tokyo

Series Editor Corey Field
Cover photograph: Peter Schaaf
Cover design: Stahl Advertising

Portions of the chapter *Beginning a Career* first appeared in
Keyboard Classics Magazine. Used by Permission.

The Robert Schumann aphorisms are from *On Music and Musicians* by Robert Schumann,
translated by Paul Rosenfeld. Copyright 1946 by Pantheon Books, Inc. Reprinted by
permission of Pantheon Books, a division of Random House, Inc.

The Chopin works are reprinted with the kind permission of Universal Edition, Vienna

The Robert Schumann lithograph on page 67 courtesy of the German Information Center, New York City

Printed on acid-free permanent paper

Contents

Introduction

The relationship of student to teacher is one of the most valuable links in our society. A computer screen full of information can never reflect the human face of a music teacher to a student. So while I know there is no substitute for the living, breathing personal connection, I hope this book may provide some insight into the realm of the study of music, and to give encouragement to the music teachers - that harried band of missionaries who carry their precious light into the world.

The Philosophy of Practising

*"I think of practising like digging a ditch. Every morning I take out
my shovel and remove a little bit of dirt..."*

Rudolf Serkin

When my revered teacher, Rudolf Serkin said this to me, I was 18 years old. For such a great pianist to express such humble sentiments about his own work was incredible to me. But now I understand what he meant.

Practising involves dedication - a devotion to the study of music itself is an integral part of what a musician does. It is something you learn when you are young, and it grows into a way of life which you cannot do without when you are older.

If you have been granted good habits and a loving attitude towards music, it becomes a necessity, like air.

There are many different kinds of practising. My own experience as a pianist has taught me that every day is different, and one of the best things you can do is to recognize within yourself what kind of work can best be done.

Sometimes it's good to play something through, or read new music. Sometimes it's better to go slowly and go over details. Sometimes it's better NOT to practise at all. We each have our own inner needs which we must listen to, and learn to obey.

Mere hours of drudgery do not accomplish anything. Endless, mindless practising is like wallpaper - repetitive decoration - unless your whole being is engaged in the process, you are wasting your time.

You must be available to the work. Set aside time for it every day - preferably the best hours of the day, when your mind is fresh, when you can learn the most.

For me, it is the morning. I do not allow anything or anyone to interfere with those hours. If I do, I am lost. I am a hermit until my first hours of practising are done. Then I may do errands, leave my studio for a short breather, but I quickly return to finish my work, and only then turn to other things.

You may find the evening hours to be better, but whatever suits you, these hours must be protected at all costs.

Privacy is essential. Make sure you are not disturbed. Practise in a room with a door on it. Put a DO NOT DISTURB sign on your door if necessary. Don't expect to be able to concentrate if you are in a room where people can easily walk in. Family members must understand that you are concentrating - otherwise they may feel free to interrupt you.

In my travels, I have found an amazing lack of awareness about what it means to concentrate while practising the piano. Friendly people seem to appear out of nowhere when I am practising. They station themselves next to the piano and try to strike up a friendly conversation or just ask to stay and listen while I practise. This is a NO-NO!. It's hard to tell people to leave you alone - when they really mean no harm.

Before a concert, I like to practise in a small room, so I know I can be alone. A concert hall with many entrances leads to socializing, and I'd rather do that after the concert - not before.

Knowing when to stop or take a break is just as important as knowing when to pour on the steam and keep going. One learns the inner signals and obeys them. To go against them is not to accomplish much. The point is to learn how to be economical in the use of time.

Discipline is essential. Turning away from the "wonderful world of entertainment" we live in to inhabit a sphere of quiet study is a struggle. Discipline is absolutely necessary in order to accomplish anything in music, although it goes against the grain of most people's lives.

I shall never forget the great Pablo Casals' admonition to his students at Marlboro: "Freedom with order," he would shout incessantly at rehearsals. Freedom means the ability to express yourself on a musical instrument without impediment. The only way to achieve this freedom comes from years of work developing your musicianship.

If it sounds endless, it is, but that is precisely the point. You never reach your goal as a musician - especially if you are a professional. Studying is a way of life if music is your life.

I don't mean to discourage anyone... only to explain that the process itself is important, and it can give you enormous satisfaction. Establishing good work habits is an essential part of being a musician, professional or amateur. It has nothing to do with talent.

More on Practising:

If you aren't listening to yourself with pleasure and interest - STOP! Practising should be dynamic and interesting - NEVER boring.

If anything begins to hurt you, STOP! You must listen to yourself - musically, and otherwise - to achieve good results. If you are uncomfortable in any way - STOP!

Practising can be a pleasurable, interesting, and unpredictable activity. Make the most of your time, and go to it!

Warming Up I: Scales

Warming up is a very individual part of practising. I have never been good at warm-up exercises, but I know it is a good idea to begin with a certain routine. When I was a child, my first teacher, my mother, gave me Hanon and Pischna exercises, but I have no actual memory of them. These studies were all written down in notebooks my mother would keep for me, so I can see exactly what I used to practise in those days (see p. 53).

I was quickly bored by finger exercises - *that I know*! There are many wonderful ways of warming up without being a drudge. For example, there are beautiful ways of playing scales - making them really interesting: scales in thirds, scales in sixths - playing them slowly, steadily, with a specific touch or dynamic in mind.

You can play a scale in so many different, intriguing ways - they are important building blocks to technique, because they are like the alphabet in a language. Pianists need to know every scale in every key, every fingering must be automatic. A good warmup is to play beautiful scales for a while - with varieties of touch and dynamics - but always with a goal in mind.

While I was studying at the Curtis Institute, I landed a summer job as a staff pianist at the Meadowmount School of Music in Elizabethtown, New York. During those years, virtually every promising young violinist alive came to Meadowmount to study with the great Ivan Galamian.

Playing for violin lessons at Meadowmount gave me a rare inside look at what makes a string player tick - and how to best serve their needs when making music together. I learned how to match sound with them, how to phrase with them, how each string player needs comfortable support from a pianist. A whole new world opened up for me by living and working in this community.

I also learned a great deal of the violin repertoire - not a bad thing for a pianist to know. To this day, you could ask me to play the orchestra part of almost any violin concerto, and I can do it. I also had a wonderful time playing with so many gifted young violinists - most of whom are well-known artists today.

Although I am not much of a violinist, I certainly learned a lot that summer. For one thing, Mr. Galamian's students were required to play scales. All of them learned the routine of practising their scales in a specific way, with certain bowings, progressing from one key to another. I have adapted this procedure to the piano to improve control of *legato* and command of dynamics across the entire keyboard. It is my own way of making something expressive and musical out of a scale. Listen to the music you can make with the suggested changes in dynamics. If you can stay involved, this is not drudgery.

Begin *pianissimo sempre*, then try varying the dynamics within each key:

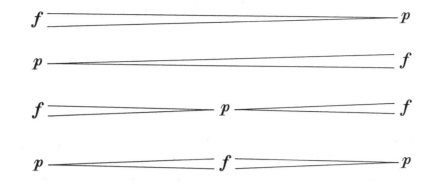

C Major

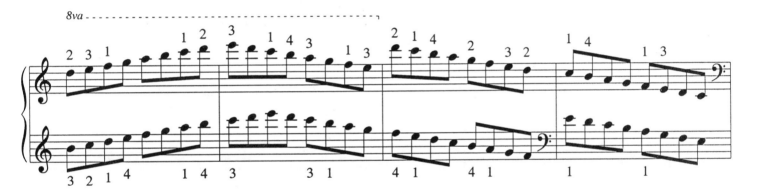

C Minor (harmonic)

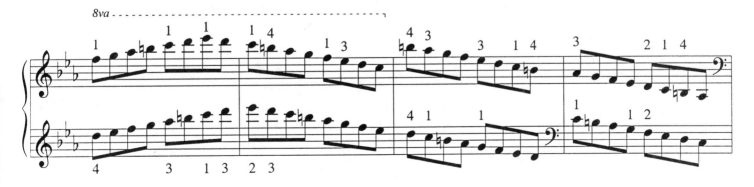

D flat Major

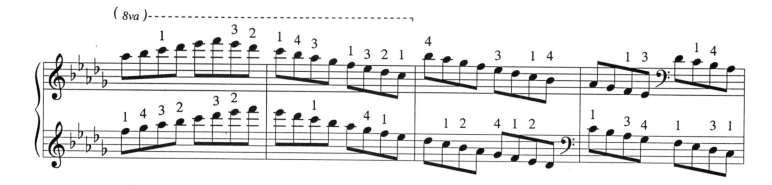

C sharp minor (harmonic)

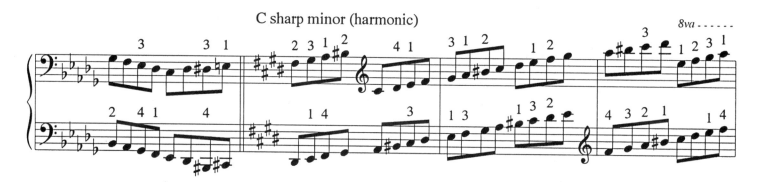

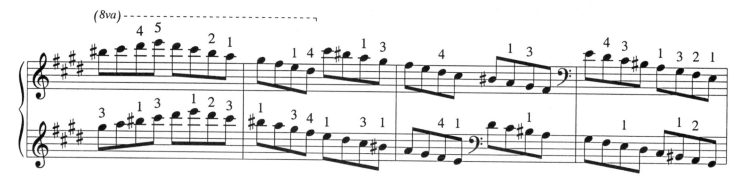

D Major

etc.

Warming Up II: Chopin

I love to warm up with Chopin. When Chopin was only 19, he wrote to his friend, Titus Woyciechowski, from Warsaw, "I have composed a study in my own manner," and later in the same year, "I have written some studies: in your presence I would play them well." What a colossal understatement!

These incomparably important works hold the key to piano technique, but they are often simply beautiful music. Select an Etude of Chopin, use it for a specific purpose, and enjoy the music along the way.

For example, the Etude Opus 10 Number 1 in C Major is like calisthenics for the fingers. I'd take this Etude and practice it slowly, watching exactly how the fingers work and how they feel. You gain strength, confidence, and facility from working on such a difficult piece - especially if you are not concerned with performing it or even playing it up to tempo. It is a wonderful warmup exercise.

The Chopin Preludes are shorter and often a little easier. My favorite warmups consist of a selection of Chopin Etudes and Preludes which give me a variety of touch and technical challenges. This sequence is musically satisfying for me, but you can choose whatever suits you!

Here is my suggestion for a typical daily warmup of Chopin:

Etude Opus 10 Number 1 in C major: This is one of the hardest of all the Chopin Etudes. I'd never want to play it in public, but used strictly as a warmup it is wonderful. Begin playing slowly, but watch the right hand and look for the most comfortable way of playing those stretches. This Etude builds strength and stamina. If you are adventurous, play it through slowly as written. Then play the whole Etude with the left hand playing the right hand part. Use only the left hand at this point. This is really a strengthening exercise, like using a Nautilus machine. Not for wimps! Go slow!

Etude Opus 10 Number 4 in C# Minor: Slowly, comfortably, no speed - just make sure both hands are comfortable and independent.

Etude Opus 10 Number 12 in C Minor ("Revolutionary"): Play this all-too familiar etude slowly, as if you've never heard it before. Each hand has its own work to do. Watch the independence of motion. Do not play fast! This pumps the blood into your hands and arms - It should feel great.

Etude Opus 25 Number 8 in D flat Major (in sixths): The contrary motion of the sixths should be comfortable. Watch and listen to coordinate each hand *molto legato*. Play without pedal and make it sound beautiful anyway.

Etude Opus 25 Number 9 in G flat Major ("Butterfly"): The upward motion of the left hand is fun after all the legato playing of the previous etudes. Relax the right hand. Discover how you can do this by observing exactly what motion is necessary and what feels good. Don't strain.

Etude Opus 25 Number 2 in F Minor: This is a contrasting touch to the "Butterfly" etude. Play very quietly and lightly. The rotary motion of the right hand should feel wonderful. The left hand does the same thing twice as slowly. This is good exercise for the wrists and fingers.

Etude Opus 25 Number 3 in F Major: You can really let go in this one. Throw both hands in opposite directions - relax, let go. This is a good releasing action which also strengthens the fifth fingers of both hands.

Prelude Opus 28 Number 24 in D Minor: The big leaps in the left hand are like jumping on a trampoline. Enjoy the distances - feel your way with a comfortable tempo. The right hand scales are invigorating. If necessary, play each hand separately at first then combine the two.

Prelude Opus 28 Number 16 in B flat Minor: This is a showpiece which would require endless drudgery if you wanted to perform it. I prefer to use it strictly as a study. Getting all these active, dangerous leaps under your belt is a real achievement, and the chromatic right hand passages may require hands-alone practise, but it's worth it!

Now you can begin your day's work...

Etude Opus 10 Number 1 in C Major

F. Chopin

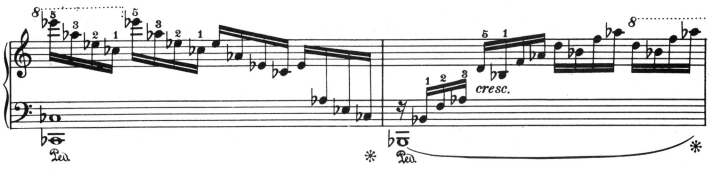
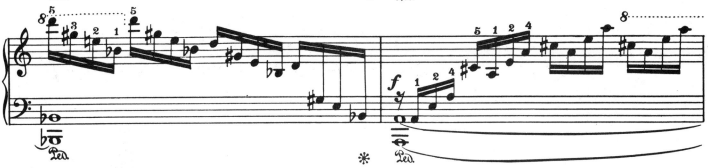

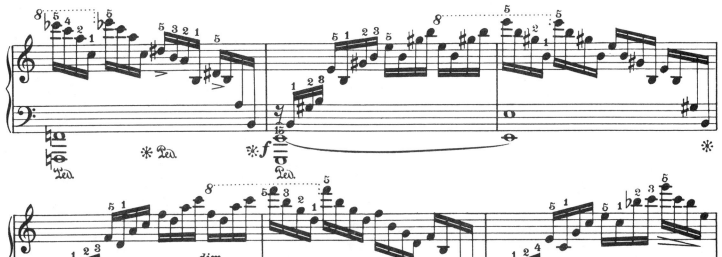

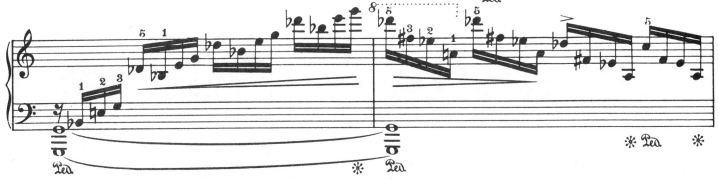

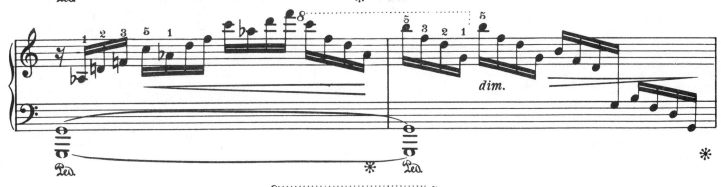

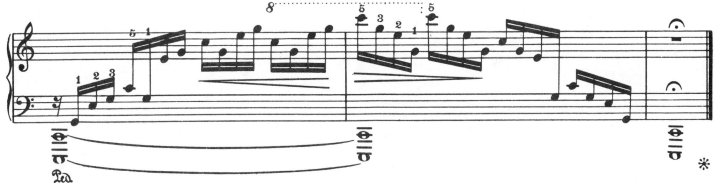

Etude Opus 10 Number 4 in C# Minor

F. Chopin

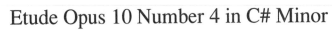

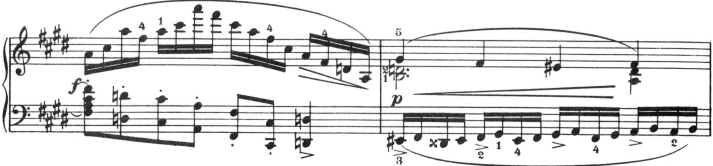

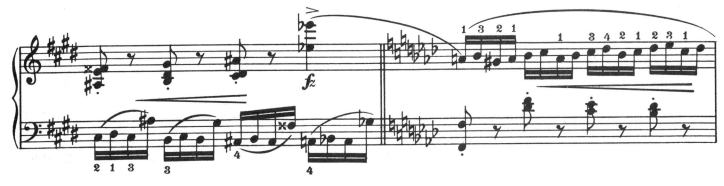

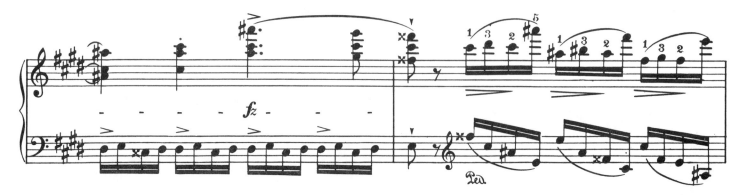

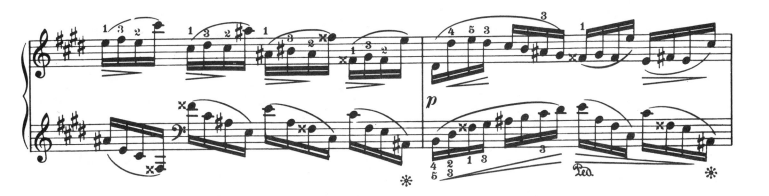

Etude Opus 10 Number 12 in C Minor ("Revolutionary")

F. Chopin

Allegro con fuoco. ($\quad$ = 160.)

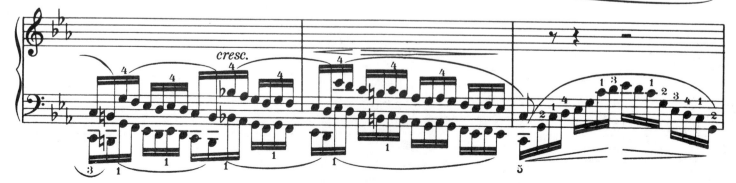

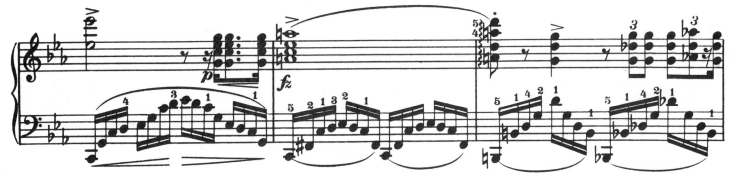

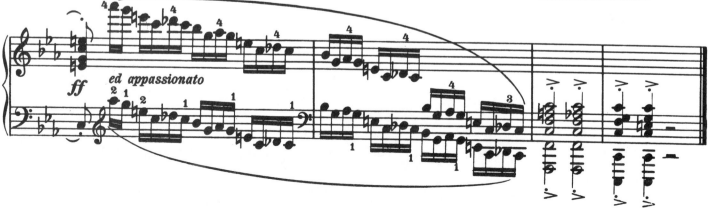

Etude Opus 25 Number 8 in D flat Major

F. Chopin

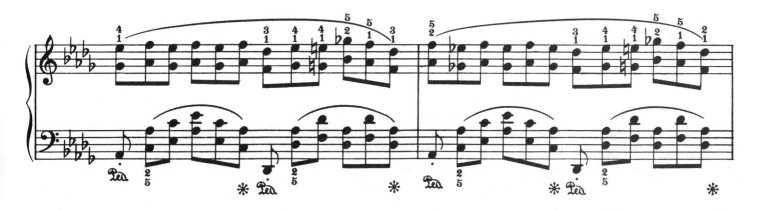

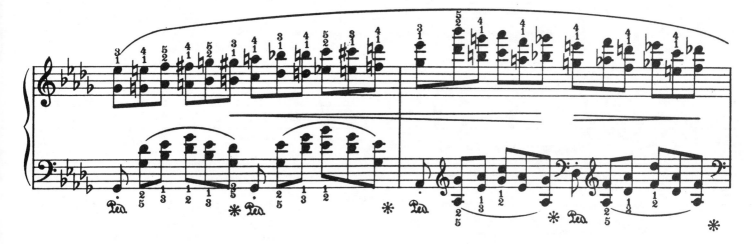

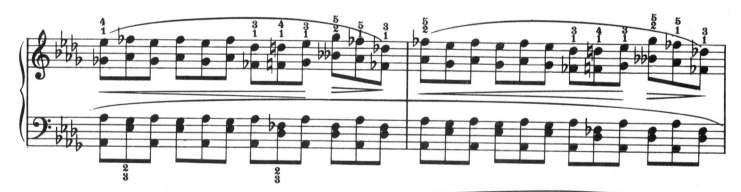

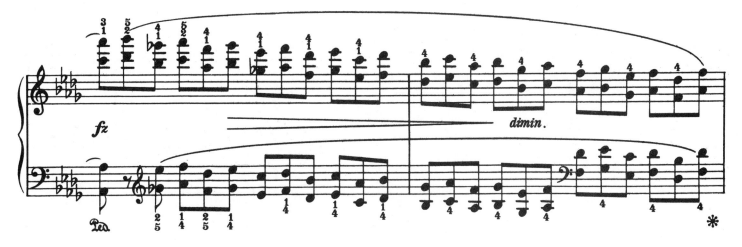

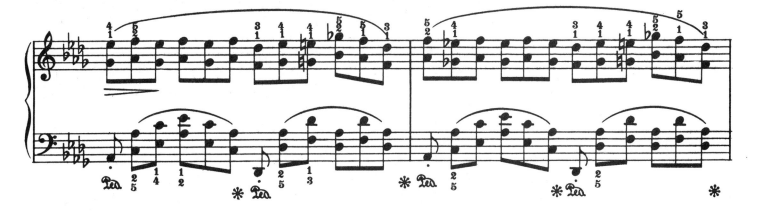

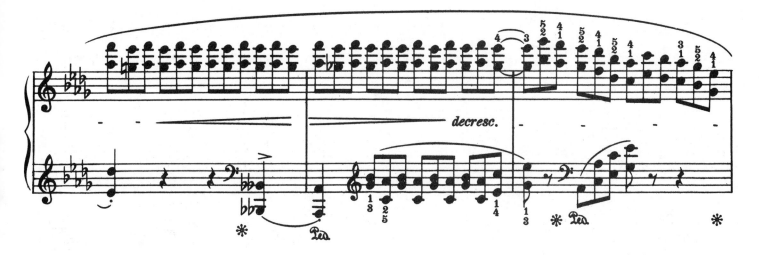

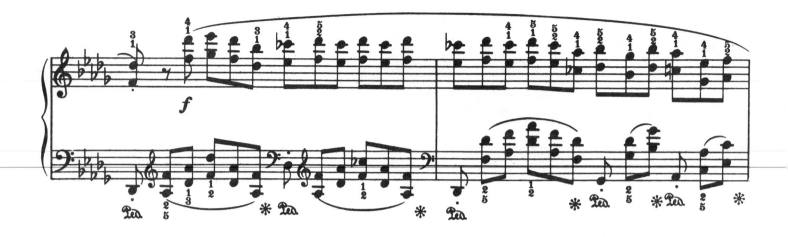

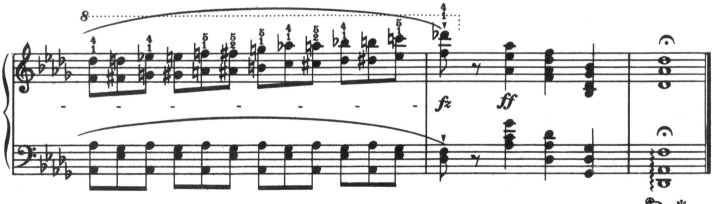

Etude Opus 25 Number 9 in G flat Major ("Butterfly")

F. Chopin

Etude Opus 25 Number 2 in F Minor

F. Chopin

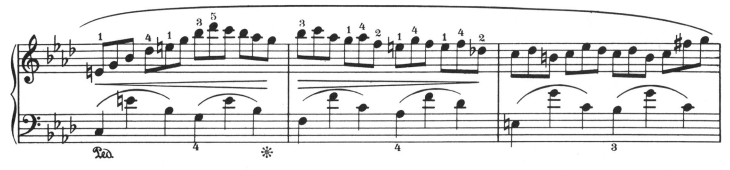

Etude Opus 25 Number 3 in F Major

F. Chopin

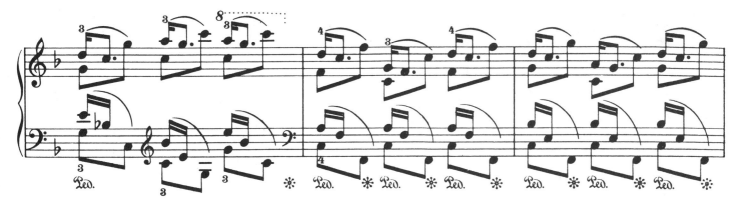

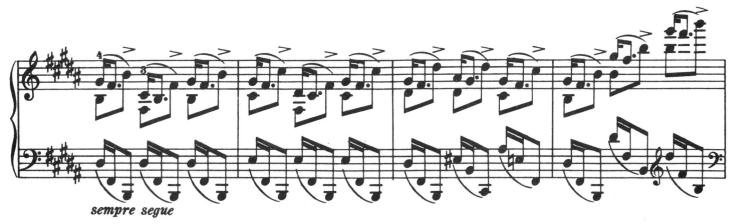

sempre segue

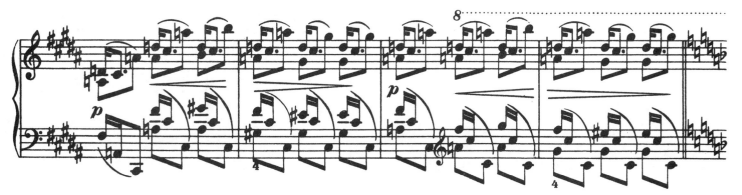

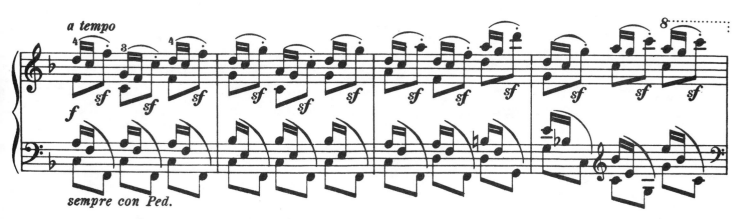

sempre con Ped.

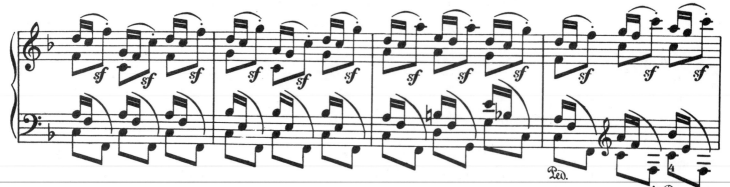

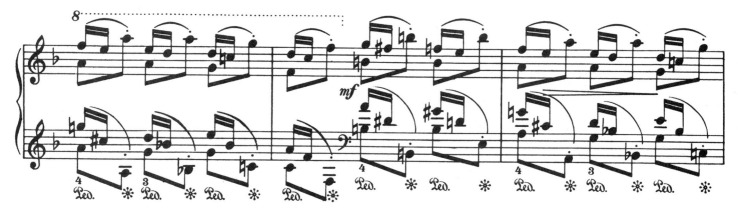

Prelude Opus 28 Number 24 in D Minor

F. Chopin

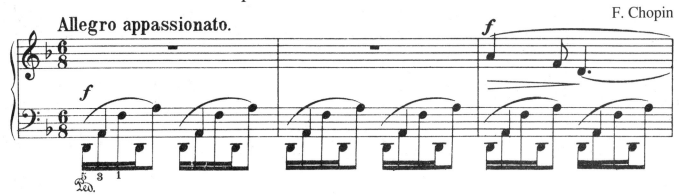

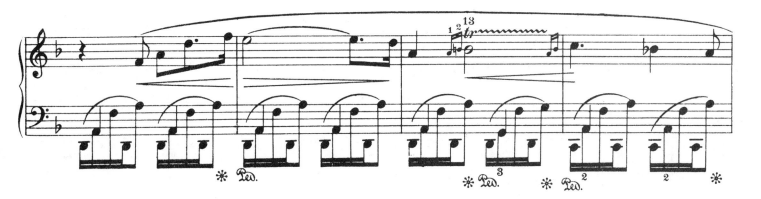

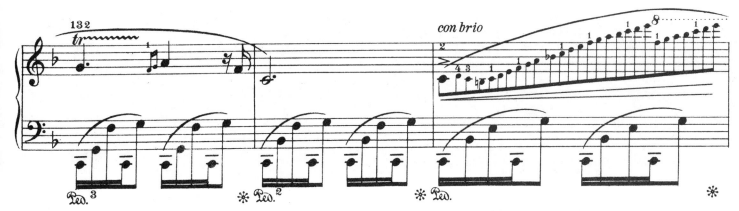

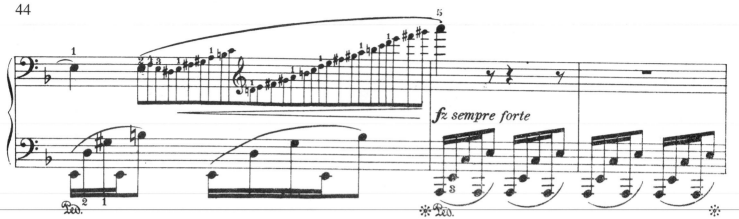

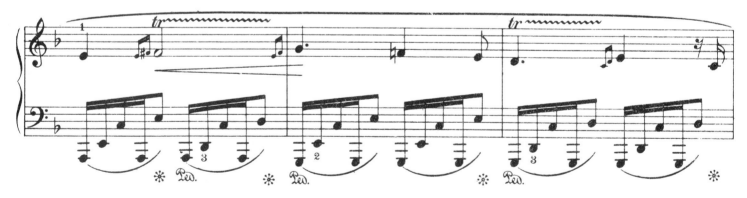

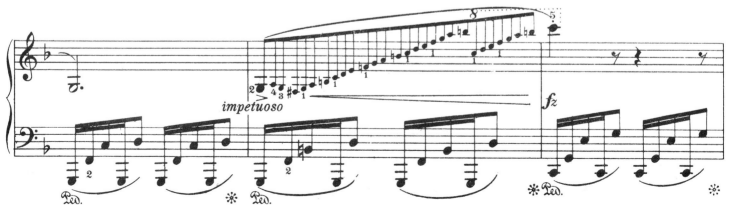

Prelude Opus 28 Number 16 in B flat Minor

F. Chopin

Presto con fuoco.

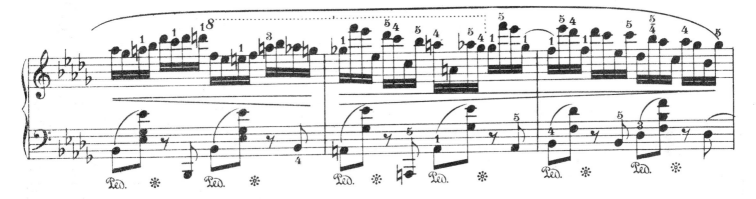

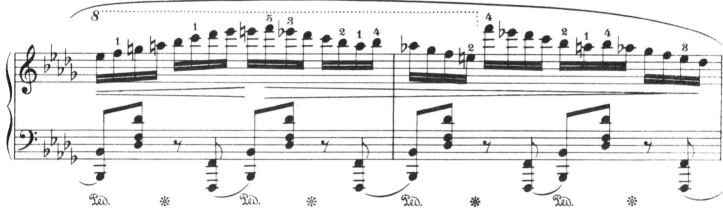

49

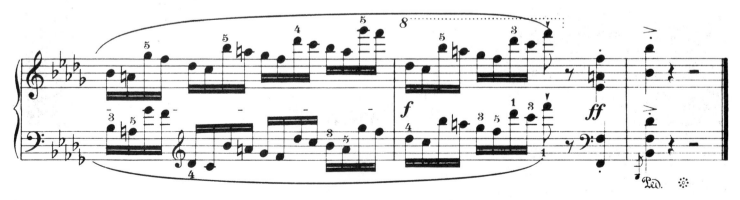

How I Became a Pianist

I'm certain that my love of music came at an early age. My mother was a piano teacher who gave lessons in our living room. Most of her students were children. Naturally, I gravitated to the piano. I seem to have walked up to the keyboard one day, tapping out "God Bless America" by ear. This may sound unusual, but to me it was quite natural - like speech.

My father was an English teacher with a great love of Shakespeare. As a child, I saw *Hamlet, A Midsummer Night's Dream*, and attended many concerts with my parents. I was steeped in literature and music before I "knew" anything. It was the soil in which I grew...

I shall never forget the impact of a concert I attended at the age of 8 with my parents in Detroit. It was a recital by Vladimir Horowitz. It changed my life. Every seat in the cavernous Masonic Auditorium was filled, but we were lucky enough to get stage seats just a few feet away from Horowitz...What a thrill!

In the course of this colossal recital, Horowitz played seven encores - the last of which was *The Stars and Stripes Forever*. This will be permanently etched in my mind... The piano lid shook whenever he played fortissimo.

I had already been playing the piano for 5 years by the time I heard this concert. After the performance, I vowed to become a pianist. It was a turning point in my life.

Age 11 months.

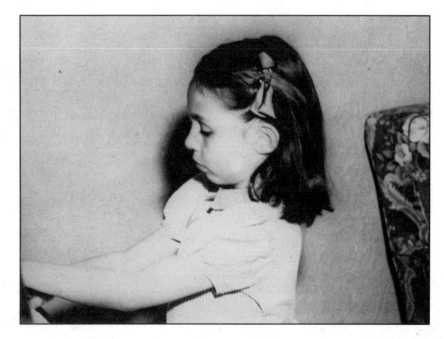

7½ years old.

52

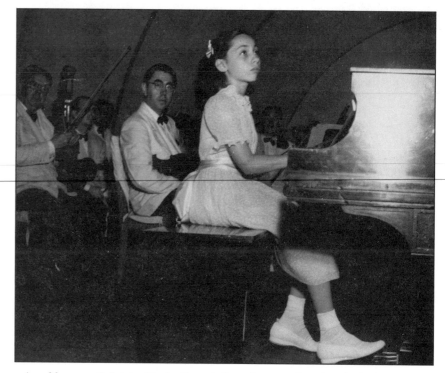

Program for my first recital.

Age 11 years: Soloist with the Detroit Symphony performing the 2nd and 3rd movements from Beethoven's Concerto Number Two in B Flat.

With my mother, 1966.

Facing page: Pages from the record book my mother kept.
Top: Her summary of my musical progress from age
20 months to 6 years.
Bottom: Lesson marks from February, 1946 including stickers
and gold stars.

Philharmonic Hall, St. Petersburg

Ruth Weakear

Ruth
Ruth Weakear
Ruth Weakear (Detroit)
135

3-4

2 0 months - recognized all current tunes

months - kept fundamental pulse by playing drum set in the piano

2¾ yrs - played - "God Bless America" by ear with R.H.
played - all pieces in Say songs - playing by ear

3 yrs old - by I. - with chords on all keys - by ear -
listening to my teaching - Cuprole
sang - first & secondary tones ① Beethoven Sonata
① Schubert Symph. 7th - after overhearing
a pupil take a lesson - found

3½ yr - played all pieces in Jones - Phythmip
4 yrs - by I - all given by ear - copied my playing/action
began reading simple pieces aloud (will I.C.
Had most of Wagners Vol. I - Sumpson - Vaughan that pr.

5 yrs - Entered kindergarten - played all my left meeting
classroom pieces intact with skill and so Schumann's mary Sugar
Selden's March - Shana of Handel - Humeresno Goldsmith
skipping - hopping "music" etc.
screamed - she had perfect pitch
Played on small organ our school auditorium with I.V
in kindergarten ① Bach minuet in G   ① Bach Polka in C
(we will Compand Clarabel).
Beethoven Sonatina in G
Ell march - Springfield

6 yrs - Mother began giving more rhythm & action instruction
to Ruth. Always holds if which she is natural good
Note reading - Scales - Sczany Vol. I
Rachiner

(use of the metronome

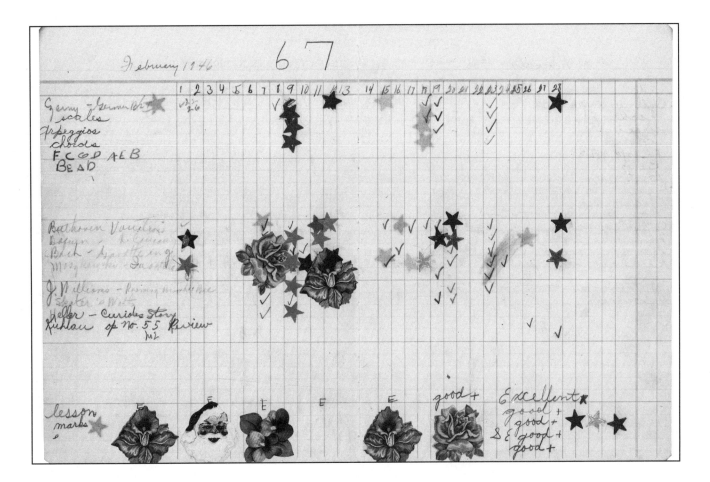

February 1946   6 7

The Background for Becoming a Musician

My mother, Miriam Meckler, created my earliest attitudes about the piano. She made studying music into a game - performing was natural, and fun. I never felt I "had" to practise - I wanted to, because it was enjoyable. What a wonderful gift my mother gave to me!

She also recognized when it was time for me to study with someone else. My mother had studied with a prominent, but somewhat intimidating, teacher in Detroit. She wanted a different kind of experience for me. I owe her so much for choosing Edward Bredshall. He was a man of humor and exuberance, a marvelous, cultivated, intellectual who had studied in Paris with Nadia Boulanger. Sometimes I'd spend the entire day with him. He was interested in art, opera, politics, everything under the sun. There were times I went for a piano lesson and didn't even play a note.

He knew the piano literature profoundly and was innovative in his programs. For example, he once gave a memorable recital composed of all the Debussy Etudes - a rare idea in those days.

On Saturday mornings he liked to gather his students together for Concerto Class. Each of us would play a concerto, with Mr. Bredshall heroically performing all the orchestra parts at a second piano. We'd discuss the music thoroughly, but Mr. Bredshall discouraged direct criticism of the playing itself. He was giving us invaluable experience as performers and colleagues. The Saturday morning sessions would culminate in two Concerto Evenings at the Detroit Institute of Arts auditorium. By then, we were already seasoned performers. My teacher created a lively, healthy atmosphere in which to study. The concerts were a breeze.

Mr. Bredshall challenged me in a very unorthodox way when I was 11. He would often make me a bet that I couldn't play huge difficult works by Prokofieff, Bartok, or Stravinsky. Naturally, I would rise to the occasion and bring in the dreaded composition fully memorized. He was as good as his word - and would pay me in cash. What a brilliant psychologist he was!

Mr. Bredshall also insisted upon tossing all kinds of new music at me to sight-read. No matter what I had prepared for my lesson I inevitably found myself playing something I had never heard before. This was a "trial by fire" which has always stood me in good stead.

Chamber Music

I fail to understand why some people consider it unusual to insist upon chamber music experience for solo pianists. Of all people, soloists need it the most! I can't imagine my playing without the years of trios, duos, ensembles, quartets, woodwind classes, choral rehearsals, voice classes, violin and cello lessons at the Curtis, at Marlboro, and at the Meadowmount School of Music. The idea of practising only the solo repertoire is unthinkable and unbearable in its isolation.

Not only is it more fun to make music with others, chamber music does wonders for your musicianship. Inevitably your pianistic palette will be enriched by the colors of the other instruments. Matching tone quality and phrasing with strings and winds on a regular basis is the best way I know to prepare for playing a concerto with orchestra. If you are accustomed to working with many different instruments, a concerto becomes second nature - it is just a big piece of chamber music.

The lack of chamber music experience is evident when a soloist performs as if the orchestra were a mere accompaniment. Great music-making can happen only when people really listen to each other, as if they were members of a string quartet.

Giving a Concert

A good concert is the crowning achievement of any pianist. It's what we all look forward to, but I think the preparation and the goals aren't always properly understood by the pianist or by the public. A concert can teach you more about yourself and about the music than 10 lessons or 100 hours in the practise room.

Preparation for a concert involves months, even years of study, depending on your age and ability and the kind of experience you've had as a pianist. For a professional, this is also true. I am sometimes amazed at how little the public knows about what it takes to play a concert. People continue to ask me "Do you still have to practise?"

I'd say that giving a concert is more likely to be understood if you explain it in terms of a sporting event. Most people know that athletes must train constantly to be prepared to compete. A pianist needs to be in training all year long, to be physically and musically fit to enter the arena of the concert stage.

I remember Mr. Serkin advised me to practise until I was exhausted, and then do one more hour. Why? So that I would not get tired while I was on stage. I took his advice while I was studying at Curtis, and it worked. My physical and mental stamina increased noticeably. I knew then I could cope with fatigue and stress while performing because I had actually been training to achieve endurance. It's like "no pain, no gain" for marathon runners, but I wouldn't suggest this for everybody. I'd never recommend such a plan for young students. This was my teacher's specific advice to me, and it worked marvelously.

The Day of the Concert

The day of a concert is a different day from any other. You must give yourself a chance to be quiet, relaxed and comfortable on that day, if at all possible.

A concert makes special demands on a performer's energy. Allow yourself plenty of time for sleep, good strengthening food, and the kind of quiet relaxation no other day provides. A concert is a special occasion, even for a professional.

I usually spend the day of a concert like this:

I get up late... have a good breakfast, go to practise, but not too much. I generally play through each piece once - lightly, not really practising, but trying out various passages from the program. By the day of the concert it is too late to change anything. The mind cannot absorb a different fingering or tempo on short notice. Use it for the next one!

After 1 or 1½ hours of playing through my program, I have lunch, usually alone - but not necessarily. Then I take a nap. On the day of a concert I can actually fall asleep for about an hour and wake up refreshed. On other days, I do not feel the need to sleep at all.

I like to go for a jog in the late afternoon, which is my usual routine anyway. I take a shower, have a steak, then go to the concert hall early to get myself into the mood. It may be necessary to try the piano in the hall just before the concert, because the tuner often comes at the last minute. I try the acoustics briefly again, then I go back to my dressing room and wait for the audience to arrive.

Nerves

My first memory of a "big" concert was at the age of 11. I played Beethoven's Piano Concerto No. 2 with The Detroit Symphony at a summer concert. As I waited in the wings, someone asked me an odd question; "Aren't you nervous?" I thought to myself, "What does that mean?" I really had no idea at the time.

I ambled out onto the stage in my blue party dress and my patent leather shoes, faced an audience of 10,000 people, and played my concerto. I never stopped to worry - it was such fun! Only later in my life did I begin to understand what "being nervous" was all about.

Children are full of confidence - they haven't yet learned to doubt themselves. Our childish innocence inexorably gives way to mature uncertainty, and so we begin to suffer from "nerves."

Every performer I know confronts some form of nervousness whenever he faces an audience. I certainly do! There is no escaping it. Eliminating nerves isn't a realistic goal for me; learning how to cope with the situation is what I've tried to accomplish.

Being prepared helps. You must know your material one thousand percent. Every time you practise or perform a piece, it is like money in the bank: experience you can store away for next time. Believe me, you make withdrawals at the concert!

Observe what happens to you before, during and after a performance. Sometimes you can learn how to avoid some of the fear by identifying the symptoms. The undeniable reality is that a concert causes physical and emotional stress. Changes in the heartbeat, pulse, all sorts of reactions are normal - even for the pro. Learning how to live with these symptoms is part of being a performer.

I can tell you one thing: No matter what tempo you have planned for, the performance will go faster... guaranteed. This means you must prepare at a slower tempo before the concert.

Your perceptions just before going onstage are often distorted. Try not to worry about what comes to your mind just before you go out there. Rationally, you have done everything you can to prepare. Now you must put yourself in the lap of the gods - and just do it! Why else would singers wish each other, *"in boca lupo"* (in the mouth of the wolf) before a performance? This is an intense, demanding, but marvelous experience. You need preparation, fortitude, *and* luck!

Beginning a Career

The plight of a pianist fresh out of music school is a difficult one at best. Assuming you are musically gifted, emotionally suited for a career and prepared with sufficient repertoire, you are still in a tough spot. As you may have noticed, the world is not waiting to hear you play. Regardless of your merits, there is no guarantee that performance opportunities will ever materialize. How do you begin?

A common starting point is to enter as many competitions as possible. If you are young enough and tough enough, I see nothing wrong with doing this, as long as you know that it may not prove a thing. (This writer auditioned for the Leventritt, Naumberg, and Queen Elizabeth of Belgium Competitions and never won a single prize in any of them.)

It is good practise for a young musician to test his mettle under the pressure of competitions: you must prepare certain repertoire, often in a limited time, and you must play under stress; both are real situations in a professional career.

However, as a musician, you must always keep in mind that competitions are a means to an end and not an end in themselves. If you have something to say and you are a true artist, it is possible that you will not be selected as a winner. The music is what counts, and you must be strong enough to keep your ideals intact no matter who wins or loses. Don't be heartbroken if you lose or too confident if you win. Life has a strange way of sorting things out in ways you can never anticipate.

Winning a competition can be a double-edged sword. A brilliant young artist may not be psychologically ready for what lies ahead after the contest is won. Imagine the ordeal of performing with a major symphony orchestra in one of the world's great concert halls with the full spotlight of public attention focused on you. Can you picture how it might feel to play a new concerto for the first time and the orchestra is the New York Philharmonic or Boston Symphony? You have no safety net, no fall-back position. If your playing isn't up to your highest standards, do you think the public or the press will be forgiving? Winning a major competition can be a great opportunity or a ticket to oblivion. So be forewarned!

Sometimes those who attain lesser prizes are winners in the long run, for they are granted time to develop at their own pace. These careers are often the long-lasting ones, while the so-called winners enjoy only fleeting attention. Their presence in the spotlight will soon be vacated by next year's first prize winners.

Although the road is not clearly visible, there are other ways to embark upon a career. For example, if you can find a special area of repertoire you feel comfortable with, and you can convince a sympathetic record company to take a chance on you, it can be a very valuable experience. That is how I received my first bit of national recognition. The Scriabin project for Connoisseur way back in 1970 was my own idea from the beginning. I strongly believed in this music and knew that no one had ever recorded all ten Scriabin Sonatas before. I was turned down by several record companies before Connoisseur decided to take a chance on me. The favorable response from reviewers around the country convinced them to go ahead with the complete set of ten Sonatas, and this in turn led CBS Masterworks to invite me to record the complete solo works of Rachmaninoff a few years later. So you see - you never can tell!

Having a manager is a by-product of having a career, not the other way around. There are plenty of pianists with managers and no careers, so to have a manager is not really a guarantee. This is a world of supply and demand. Ask yourself: "What do I have to offer that is special and why should anyone want to buy a ticket to hear me play?" This question may sound absurd, but in the music business, people have to want to buy what you have to sell. Commercial considerations do exist, and we must learn to cope with them.

Thirty or forty years ago, when a young artist graduated from a conservatory, he would rent Town Hall and play his New York debut. In those days, there was a lot more curiosity about young artists, a larger audience for solo recitals, and six or seven newspapers in New York City alone. Today you face a different situation. There are fewer opportunitites for solo recitals, more public interest in chamber music, and very few newspapers! You are lucky if you even attain a review of your concert, and if it is favorable, what then? The field is strewn with young musicians who have made "successful" New York debuts and still find themselves no closer to achieving their dreams.

What other path can you take? I'd say it is a wonderful idea to play a great deal of chamber music for musical, social and life-enhancing reasons. There is far too much solitude in the life of any classical pianist.

You have to remember that making a concert career is a lifetime proposition. You may never be catapulted to fame with an auspicious debut, but if you hope to have a life in music, it is healthier to play and study music with people you enjoy; teach, play anything and everything you can; start your own series; participate in festivals at any level available to you; audition for anyone and everyone who will hear you.

The road is unpredictable but the destination is worth the effort. I wish you good luck.

Great Teachers I: Rudolf Serkin

I first came to Mr. Serkin when I was a teenager attending a summer music camp in the Berkshires. One of my counselors, the violinist Berl Senofsky, knew Serkin and had been to Marlboro, which at the time was a small summer music colony at an obscure New England college. Berl thought it would be an excellent experience for me to play for Mr. Serkin, so he called him and arranged for an audition. I blush to confess that I wasn't quite sure who Rudolf Serkin was, but I trusted Senofsky's judgement.

For several weeks I prepared the works I was to play, including pieces by Bach, Chopin, and the Beethoven Sonata Opus 101 in A Major (again, ignorance was bliss) and I eagerly anticipated the car trip from Stockbridge to Marlboro, Vermont. When I first drove onto the grounds of Marlboro College, I was enchanted by its rustic informality. I remember seeing the pianist, Anton Kuerti, leaning on a broom, about to sweep the dining room which doubled as a concert hall in those days.

I had no inkling that my afternoon at Marlboro would alter my life forever, that my high-spirited, easy-going attitude towards music would be profoundly affected by this man whom I had never seen before. Outwardly, Rudi was warm, welcoming, friendly. His easy grin hid eyes behind impenetrably thick glasses. Not knowing enough to be afraid, I breezed through the program for him. I heard him say some good things about my Bach and Chopin ("I can see that you play like a tiger.") and some ambiguous remarks about my Beethoven Sonata.

The point is that after playing for Serkin, I could never go back to being the ignorant little girl that I had been the day before. Because he said he would like to take me as a student at the Curtis Institute, my life immediately changed course.

Studying with one of the world's great artists is an awesome experience. It was fortunate for me that I did not quite grasp this at the time. Rudi was my teacher and I liked him. When I think of it now, studying with Serkin was like jumping into the ocean. My immense inexperience was like a life preserver keeping me afloat.

During my Curtis days, Mr. Serkin played a great number of concerts all over the world. He performed often in Philadelphia with Eugene Ormandy. Imagine the thrill of hearing performances by your very own teacher of works you were experiencing for the first time: the Brahms B Flat, the "Emperor," the Brahms D Minor with the glorious Philadelphia Orchestra. The impact was staggering and unforgettable.

Rudi made me look for musical concepts I had never thought to consider before. He made me listen to my sound. He challenged me to find a way to develop tonal control and a wide range of dynamics. He pointed out my weaknesses and admonished me to find my own way to correct them. He never imposed his way of playing upon anybody. He guided me to see what needed to be done, and I struggled mightily to find the way to achieve it.

Because Rudi was so tough on himself, we followed his example. Complete dedication to the music, fidelity to the composer became central moral beliefs that we lived by. His will was so powerful, his influence so dramatic, that it seemed unbelievable that I could ever do without him. Even so I was able to internalize these values and to continue working on my own. Thanks to Mr. Serkin, I felt capable of searching for the musical truth.

Marlboro 1964: Bach Triple concerto performance.
From left: Rudolf Serkin, Alexander Schneider, Ruth Laredo, M. Horszowski.

Great Teachers II: Johannes Brahms

Eugenie Schumann, the 7th of 8 children born to Robert and Clara Schumann, was an extremely talented pianist. In her diary, she reveals touching details of her family's life and of her musical study with Johannes Brahms.

There is nothing to compare with her personal description of Brahms as close family friend and as her very own piano teacher. She tells us "how things really had been."

This special relationship between a great artist and his sensitive young student reveals the essence of the nature of teaching. Brahms must have been the ideal teacher - his guidance of Eugenie holds many truths for us today.

I quote directly from Eugenie Schumann's memoir:

In the spring of 1872 my mother told me that she was going to ask Brahms to give me lessons during the summer. She thought that the stimulating influence of a fresh teacher might incite me to a more eager pursuit of my studies. I felt very unhappy; Mamma could not be satisfied with my progress, and I thought that I had done my best. There was no one for whom I would have worked rather than for her. Now Brahms really did come twice a week. He entered the room punctually to the minute, and he was always kind, always patient, and adapted his teaching to my capabilities and the stage of my progress in quite a wonderful way. Also he took a great deal of trouble in the training of my fingers. He had thought about such training and about technique in general much more than my mother, who had surmounted all technical difficulties at an age when one is not yet conscious of them. He made me play a great many exercises, scales and arpeggios as a matter of course, and he gave special attention to the training of the thumb, which, as many will remember, was given a very prominent part in his own playing. When the thumb had to begin a passage, he flung it on to the key with the other fingers clenched. As he kept his wrist loose at the same time, the tone remained full and round even in a *fortissimo*. Considerable time was daily given to the following exercises on the passing-under of the thumb:

Also to be played in triplets.

I had to take the note on which the thumb was used, quite lightly - so to speak, on the wing - and accentuate the first of every four notes strongly. Then I had to play the same exercise in triplets, with strong accents on the first note of every triplet. When I could play the exercises faultlessly in keys without the black notes, I played them, always beginning with the thumb, in C sharp, F sharp, A flat, E flat, and D flat.

Then followed the common chords with inversions through three or four octaves, also in groups of four notes and in triplets, beginning with the accent on the first note. When I had played this about ten times, I changed the accent to the second, then to the third note of each group, so that all the fingers were exercised equally. I practised these arpeggios alternately as triplets and groups of six, and had to distinguish clearly between the groups of twice three and three times two notes.

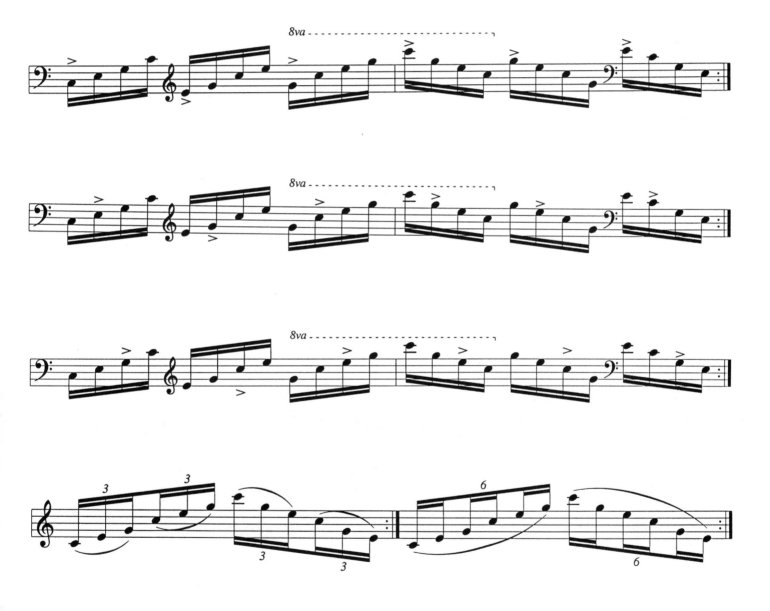

Brahms made me practise shakes also in triplets. In all exercises he made me play the non-accentuated notes very lightly. I practised the chromatic scale with the first and third, first and fourth, and first and fifth fingers, and he often made me repeat the two consecutive notes where the thumb was passed under. They were all, in fact, quite simple exercises; but carefully executed, first slowly, then more rapidly, and at last *prestissimo*, I found them extremely helpful for the strengthening, suppleness, and control of the fingers. I also played some of the difficult exercises published later as 'Fifty-one Exercises for Pianoforte by Brahms,' in which he did not include the easier and musically less valuable ones.

With regard to studies Brahms said: play easy ones, but play them as rapidly as possible. He thought very highly of Clementi's *Gradus ad Parnassum*, and made me play a great number of these.

In the study of Bach's works, Brahms laid the greatest stress on rhythm, and gave me directions which, like seeds, took root and continued their growth throughout my musical life. They greatly increased my perception of the subtleties of rhythmic movement. He made it one of the principal rules that in constantly recurring figures the accents should always be the same, and that they should be stressed not so much by strong attack as by greater pressure on the accentuated and more lightness of the non-accentuated notes.

The melodic notes of figures he made me play *legatissimo*; the harmonic, however, e.g. the notes of broken chords, quite lightly. He never wrote purely rhythmic accents in above the notes, as he held them to be an integral part of the figure; but accents specially intended, or not self-evident, he marked, to make them quite clear, and pencilled phrasing in with slurs. But I was never allowed to interpret a passage thus phrased by lifting and fresh attack of the hands; only by rhythmic emphasis and nuance.

In any work by Bach, Brahms would occasionally permit an emphatic lifting of the notes (*portamento*), but never a *staccato*. 'You must not play Bach *staccato*,' he said to me. 'But Mamma sometimes uses a *staccato* in Bach,' I demurred. Then he replied, 'Your mother's youth goes back to a time when it was the fashion to use *staccatos* in Bach, and she has retained them in a few cases.'

The seed which he sowed fell upon good soil and bore fruit in the course of years, and when I began to teach I recognised how much I owed to him. I only wish I had told him this. If I might venture upon comparison between my mother's teaching and his, I would say: My mother primarily stimulated imagination and feeling, Brahms the intellect. To have been influenced by both was perhaps the most perfect teaching imaginable.

Johannes Brahms in 1869 at age 36

Robert Schumann in 1839 at age 29

Great Teachers III: Robert Schumann on Music

"If he had never written a note of music, Robert Schumann's aphorisms, letters and essays alone would constitute a priceless legacy to mankind."
Robert Haven Schauffler in "Florestan"

Robert Schumann's considerable literary talent created an enormous output of essays, reviews, and impressions of his contemporaries. He also had a special affinity for the world of children. He and his wife Clara were the parents of 8 of them. His *House Rules and Maxims for Young Musicians* were published as a companion piece to his *Album for the Young, Opus 68*.

Here is a selection of my favorite aphorisms by Robert Schumann:

You must practise scales and other finger exercises industriously. There are people, however, who think they may achieve great ends by doing this for many hours daily, they practise mechanical exercises. That is as reasonable as trying to recite the alphabet faster and faster every day. Find a better use for your time.

"Dumb keyboards" have been invented; practise on them for a while in order to see that they are worthless. dumb people cannot teach us to speak.

Play in time! The playing of some virtuosos resembles the walk of a drunken man. do not make these your models.

Try to play easy pieces well; it is better than playing difficult ones poorly.

When you play, do not concern yourself with who may be listening.

If you have finished your daily musical work and feel tired, do not force yourself to labor further. It is better to rest than to practise without joy or freshness.

When you grow older, avoid playing what is merely fashionable. Time is precious. It would require a hundred lives merely to get acquainted with all the good music that exists.

Have an open eye for life as well as the other arts and sciences.

Art was not created as a way to riches. Strive to become a true artist; all else will take care of itself.

It is the artist's lofty mission to shed light into the very depths of the human heart.

Great Teachers IV: Clara Schumann

What could be more vivid than the personal recollection of Clara Schumann's daughter Eugenie, who listened enraptured to her mother at the piano. Eugenie's memoirs describe how Clara warmed up in the morning, what she played, and how she worked.

Such a wealth of remembrance can inspire any piano student, so I quote passages of particular delight:

> These were wonderful days, which now, on looking back, seem steeped in eternal sunshine. But the most wonderful of them was the day on which Mamma began to practise again after a fair interval of rest. Directly after breakfast the grand piano was opened and the house flooded with sound. Scales rolled and swelled like a tidal sea, *legato* and *staccato*; in octaves, thirds, sixths, tenths, and double thirds; sometimes in one hand only, while the other played accompanying chords. Then arpeggios of all kinds, octaves, shakes, everything *prestissimo* and without the slightest break, exquisite modulations leading from key to key. The most wonderful feature of this practising was that although the principle on which it was based was always the same, it was new every day, and seemed drawn ever fresh from a mysterious wellspring. Irresistible inspiration, perfect rhythm, such as springs from the souls of only the greatest artists, combined with absolute mastery of technique, made these exercises a wonderfully spiritualised achievement. A distant relative of ours, when she was staying with us, said that she had never believed the story told of Paganini, who made people weep with the playing of a scale; but that now she had heard Mamma practise, she could understand it. I do not think any one could ever have forgotten it who had heard it, even once only; and here were we children hearing it day by day. Though I was still so young, my mind was filled with inexpressible joy and satisfaction, and this has continued throughout my life, to the day when we heard it for the last time. We often pressed Mamma to write down the sequence of an hour's exercises, but she always said it was impossible to retain exactly this kind of free fantasia.
>
> After the technical exercises, which, in those years, she always ended with Czerny's *Toccata*, came the turn of Bach: either the *Italian Concerto*, or several fugues from the *Wohltemperierte Klavier*, the great fugue in A minor, *Chromatic Fantasia*, the Organ Fugue in A minor arranged for piano by herself, and sometimes Partitas or Suites. finally Schumann's *Toccata* and five or six studies by Chopin. She never practised in the sense usually attached to the word. I have never heard my mother practise slowly, bar by bar. She had overcome all technical difficulties when she was a child, and grown up with the new creations of Chopin, Mendelssohn, and Schumann, with those of Thalberg, Henselt, and Liszt. She had made herself acquainted with all these works immediately on their appearance. Now only those of Brahms were new to her, and to these she

gave the right interpretation at first sight, without preliminary study. She penetrated so deeply into the spirit of each work, that they became almost part of her. They lay enshrined in her soul, and when she drew them forth they seemed to have been newly created. As a rule she practised without the music. I remember a few occasions when I came into the room while she was at work; she asked me to find her the music in order to verify some point or other. We never disturbed Mamma without good cause when she was at the piano, but we knew that we might come in at any time, and that she even liked it. She always gave us a kind glance whenever we entered the room. I used to wonder at the time that she could go on playing so unconcernedly while she talked to us of other things. While she played scales she would often read letters open on the desk in front of her.

When she went into her room after breakfast, the first thing she did was to open the piano, one of us dusted it, and it remained open all day. She usually played for an hour after breakfast, and again in the late afternoon towards twilight.

She also wished me to practise for three hours daily... she herself taught me twice a week for an hour in the mornings. She kept to these hours with the greatest regularity, no matter what demands were made upon her. I remember my first lesson most distinctly. It began, like all the subsequent ones, with scales and arpeggios, and the first Study from Czerny's *School of Velocity* followed. I played a page of it, then my mother said, 'That is all right so far, but don't you think chords sound much nicer like this?' She played the first eight bars from the wrist with all the notes of equal strength, *forte*, yet exquisitely mellow in tone, never stiffening the wrist for an instant, and knitting the chords rhythmically together so that the simple piece suddenly took on life and character. It was a revelation to me; my feeling for beauty of touch and rhythm was stirred into life from that moment.... The study was followed by the Bach fugue in E minor from Volume 1 of the *Wohltemperierte Klavier*. I learnt strict *legato* and the subtle shading of rhythm in this... Beethoven formed the nucleus of every lesson. What had been written was sacred to her. 'Do you think Beethoven would have taken the trouble to write all this notation, dots, ties, crotchets here, quavers there, if he had meant it to be otherwise? And don't you hear for yourself that it must be so, and could not be anything else?'

'And now we must work at some of Papa's music,' she said... 'and I would like to start you with the *Jugend Album*.' So we took each of these little gems one by one in their proper order, and I remember every word the beloved teacher said about them. These pieces would teach me rhythm and characterisation; underlying ideas I might supply myself. 'Whatever your father did, saw, read, would at once shape itself into music. When he read poetry, resting on the sofa after dinner, it turned into songs. When he saw you children at play, little pieces of music grew out of your games. While he was writing down the *Humoresque*, some acrobats came along and performed in front of our house; imperceptibly the music they made stole into the composition. He was always quite unconscious of these inspirations; it would be foolish to think that he had used them intentionally as an incentive. He invented their titles after they were finished. These are quite characteristic, and might help in the interpretation, but they are not necessary.'

With regard to fingering my mother restricted her annotations as much as possible, chiefly to tie-fingering. She disapproved of fingered editions, and held that one should have acquired the right feeling for fingering through study of scales, arpeggios, and other exercises. She also did not approve of otherwise annotated editions, and unwillingly consented, after an argument with Brahms, to my using Czerny's edition of Bach's fugues. Brahms had advised it as saving me trouble, because its ample fingering facilitates the division of the parts between the two hands, which otherwise has to be picked out laboriously. He said I need not pay attention to the other annotations, of which he too disapproved.

My mother expected a good deal of me at first: a new study, a Bach fugue and prelude, part of a Beethoven sonata, and a Schumann or Chopin piece for every lesson, or at least once a week. But she soon saw that she must lower her standard. As I had only had an hour's daily practise at school, and probably had not even employed that to the best advantage, I had no technique... But if my achievements were modest, Mamma's patience was unlimited, and every small improvement was generously praised. After the lesson she gave me a kiss and dismissed me, when I took myself and my music out of her room with a light heart.

Robert and Clara Schumann
Hamburg, 1850

Eugenie Schumann in her 18th year

Ruth Laredo

Hailed as "America's first lady of the piano" (*New York Daily News*), Ruth Laredo has achieved international distinction as soloist with orchestra, chamber musician, recitalist, and recording artist. While commanding a vast repertoire ranging from Beethoven to Barber, she has been particularly acclaimed for her interpretations of works by Russian, French and Spanish composers.

She has appeared at Carnegie Hall, the Kennedy Center, the Metropolitan Museum of Art, the Library of Congress and the White House, and with such prestigious orchestras as the New York Philharmonic, the Cleveland Orchestra and the Boston Symphony.

Noted for her strong commitment to chamber music, Ms. Laredo frequently collaborates with the Tokyo and Shanghai String Quartets. She was a founding member of the Music from Marlboro Concerts, and appeared in the very first "Isaac Stern and Friends" concert at Carnegie Hall. Each season she devotes part of her schedule to performances with flutist Paula Robison.

Her recent tour of Russia, highlighted by recitals in Moscow, St. Petersburg, and Odessa, formed part of an extensive television profile of the pianist on "CBS Sunday Morning" with Charles Kuralt.

Ruth Laredo was the first pianist ever to record the complete solo works of Rachmaninoff. Her pioneering project for CBS Masterworks was chosen "Best of the Month" by *Stereo Review*, earned her a "Best Keyboard Artist" award from *Record World*, and a Grammy nomination (her third). Her passionate advocacy of Scriabin served to stimulate a revival of interest in the music of this great Russian composer.

She is Special Arts Correspondent for National Public Radio's *Morning Edition*, frequent guest critic on WQXR's *First Hearing*, and a regular columnist for *Keyboard Classics Magazine*. C.F. Peters commissioned her to edit a new Rachmaninoff Urtext Edition. The first volume containing the Ten Preludes Opus 23 and Prelude Opus 3 Number 2 inaugurated the series.

Ms. Laredo has been a member of the faculty of Yale University, the Curtis Institute, and has given master classes at the Eastman School, Indiana University, the New England Conservatory, and the Academy of the West in Santa Barbara.

She was a guest speaker at the Harvard/Radcliffe Women's Leadership conference at the John F. Kennedy School of Government; the Music Teachers National Association honored her for "Distinguished Service to Music in America," and she held the Wiley Housewright Eminent Scholar Chair during a residency at Florida State University.

Born and raised in Detroit and now living in New York City, she studied with Rudolf Serkin at the Curtis Institute of Music.